SAP SD Interview Questions, Answers, and Explanations

By SAPCOOKBOOK.COM

Please visit our website at www.sapinterviewing.com

© 2005 Equity Press all rights reserved.

ISBN 1-933804-04-1

Table of Contents

Motivation

During the course of an average project, I am usually called upon by a project manager to "help screen resources" for different parts of the project. And one thing comes to mind – if done properly, it's very time consuming, and it's really hard work!

My interviews usually sound something like this –

Jim: "Please rate yourself, on a scale of 1-10 on your SRM knowledge and experience..."

Interviewee: "Um, probably something like 10..."

Jim: "OK, so, let me just say something... I don't believe there is such a thing as a ten."

Interviewee: "What would you rate yourself?"

Jim: "I rate myself an 8."

Interviewee: "Why so low?"

Jim: "There's no such thing as a ten. All of the nines are working at SAP, SAP Labs, or SAP Consulting, and so basically that puts me at about an eight. But we're here to talk about *your* skills. And so you think you're a 10, huh? OK, so tell me what you know about debugging the n-step approval workflow..."

And then I try to ask the questions that truly flesh out a person's understanding of the software. It's part science, part art to be sure – but the #1 thing I'm looking for in an interview is that the resource represents their skills truthfully. The good resources know what they know, know what they don't know, and they're open about it.

And so I hope that this book will serve as a much-needed guide for managers trying to get the right resource for their project. If you construct an interview based on these questions, I'm confident you can get a good idea about the depth and breadth of a consultant's experiences and accumulated knowledge.

Jim Stewart

Riverside, California

December 2005

Introduction

Each interview question has a question and an answer – that is pretty straightforward – but when you see the guru icon – this is information that represents the highest degree of knowledge in a particular area. So if you're looking for a "SD guru," be sure to listen for answers similar to those given under the guru icon.

 Don't be bamboozled!

The SD Guru has spoken!

SAP SD Interview Questions, Answers, and Explanations

Question 1: Sales BOM and Delivery Group

We create an order for a sales BOM with three sub items. Since the sub item components must not be delivered without the main product we declared the main item category as delivery group. The problem arises when there is zero availability for the main item and no schedule line can be confirmed. The main item is defined as delivery group but the delivery is created without the main and only the component sub items. The delivery group becomes broken up. This occurs only in VL01N and VL10 dialogue mode. In VL10 background it works ok, so no delivery item is created at all for those unconfirmed items. How do we fix this?

A: The message is not configurable; at least in releases <= 4.6. But you can change the 'W' to an 'E' with a modification.

Question 2: Stock Transfer

How do we transfer stocks under one company code
from plant to plant?

A: Plant to plant is handled using MB1B. If stock
transfer orders with deliveries are configured, use ME27.

Question 3: Actual PGI without Stock

I can press actual PGI successfully even without stock, but I know that is the wrong way to do so. The correct scenario should have enough stock then press actual PGI. How can I configure this?

A: You must make sure you do not allow negative inventory in MM.

Question 4: Pop up in Order Creation

When I create a sales order using VA01, a pop up appears saying, "for this customer there are open quotations". I would like to disable that pop up. How would I do that?

A: You can change this by checking order header configuration (VOV8), and field quotation messages.

Question 5: Scale Price Condition

I have a fixed amount discount condition type, which I need to establish a constant discount for all possible values. For a value of $100, a discount of $3. For a value of $200, a discount of $6. For a value of $300, a discount of $9 and so on. The problem is that I cannot maintain this scale at VK11 for all possible high values. I need to determine that for each $100 there is a $3 discount. How do I configure this?

A: Follow these steps: (1) new routine in VOFM -> Formulas -> Condition value. There you divide quantity by 100, and multiply the integer part of result by 3. (2) new condition - calculate type - G-formula. (3) Input condition in your pricing procedure and input AltCTy (Condition formula for alternative calculation type) - new formula.

Question 6: VPRS Not Copied to Billing Document

I have two condition types for cost. One is customized and the other is VPRS. Their values are determined correctly in sales order. A problem arises when I create the d/o and billing document. The condition type VPRS is incorrect with value 'o,' while the customized one is correct. What is the cause of this?

A: The VPRS is a valuation condition, normally the cost of goods sold. If it comes from the material master record, it is a standard valuation price. However, if it comes from the information record, it is the very cost of goods sold. You may have a difference from the price you valued your material at and the real cost of purchase. Check if you have a standard value in your master record or if you have a relevant info record. Another possibility is your customized condition is undoing the VPRS.

Question 7: Serial Numbers in a Delivery Document

Which report will show the serial number assigned in a delivery document?

A: Take a look at function modules with SERIAL_*. For example, SERIAL_LS_PRINT.

Question 8: Condition Type and Pricing Procedure

I received the error message, "Condition type Z928 is not in procedure ZCS928 AV." How do I include the condition type Z928 in pricing procedure ZCS928?

A: Follow pathway:

SPRO ->Sales and Distribution ->Basic Functions ->Pricing ->Pricing Control -> Define and Assign Pricing Procedures

From here select "Maintain pricing procedures." Next, select procedure ZCS928, then "Control Data." Add Z928 to your procedure.

Question 9: Using Transaction Mass to Create Sales Representative

Is it possible to use transaction MASS to assign a sales representative as a partner?

A: Yes. Using the MASS transaction, select object KNA1. Then select table name KNVP.

Question 10: Serial Numbers

Where in the sale order would you enter the serial numbers for material?

A: Serial numbers are entered on the delivery document and not a sale order, as this allows for multiple serial numbers to be entered for a single line. For example, you may have 10 serial numbers for a quantity of 10.

Question 11: Variant Pricing

I need to have an additive price based on a variant characteristic selected and then provide a discount for each of the characteristics. I must discount the correlating characteristic, not the gross value.

price

Char 1 = 1.00
Char 2 = 2.00
Char 3 = 3.00

gross price = 6.00

discount

Char 1 = 10% of 1.00 = .10
Char2 = 20% of 2.00 = .40
Char3 = 15% of 3.00 = .45

total discounts = .95

The discount may vary by customer. How do I find out how configure this?

A: You can find out how to configure this by taking a look at the documentation for "$SET_PRICING_FACTOR," in LO-VC.

Question 12: Area Menu Maintenance

I'm working in SE43, area menu maintenance. I am copying an existing area menu where the name of the main node is already specified. I took standard menu COND_AV (used as standard for maintaining condition records in SD) and made its copy as ZCOND_AV. I've changed its description from "condition maintenance" to another description. However, in the area menu itself the main node still has "condition maintenance." How do I change this?

A: This can be solved through SE43 itself. Create a new menu area then the name of that area menu is automatically assigned to the main node.

Question 13: Pricing Procedure for Industrial and Domestic Customers

We have two types of customers industrial and domestic. The domestic customers have a price list. For the industrial customers, the price is calculated on basis of percentage of the cost. Since there is a possibility that industrial customers might also buy domestic products at any given point of time, we are forced to make one pricing procedure. Is there another solution?

A: You can create a VOFM subroutine (transaction code VOFM->Formulas->Condition value) and set this subroutine in your procedure as transaction code V/2 in field AltCTy (Condition formula for alternative calculation type). In the ABAP coding you can describe all of your requirements.

Question 14: Payment Method

How can I transfer the payment method from customer master to sales order automatically?

A: Use the user exit "userexit_move_field_to_vbkd" in report MV45AFZZ with this coding:

```
DATA: via LIKE knb1-zwels.
IF vbkd-zlsch IS INITIAL.
IF NOT vbak-kunnr IS INITIAL.
SELECT SINGLE zwels INTO via
FROM knb1
WHERE bukrs = vbak-bukrs_vf
AND kunnr = vbak-kunnr.
vbkd-zlsch = via(1).
ENDIF.
ENDIF.
```

Question 15: Output via Email

How can you send output through an email instead of a fax or printout?

A: Check whether the transmission medium has been maintained for the processing routines for your output type. Make sure that this transmission medium is placed in the partner functions evenly.

Follow this path:

SPRO -> SD-> Basic Functions-> output control--> output determination-> determination using condition technique-> maintain O.deter.for sales documents-> Maintain output types. Use transaction code V30.

Question 16: "Problem with bapi_salesorder_change"

We have a problem with "bapi_salesorder_change." We need to change a position in a sales order but when we fill the structures bapi does not change the sales order. What should we do?

A: You must fill the update structures properly. The order header needs to read "order_header_inx-updateflag = 'U',". The item must read "order_item_inx = 'U'." Each field touched in "order_item_in" needs to have an 'X' in the corresponding field of "order_item_inx."

Question 17: Infostructure Filling

We have two Company Codes and new Infostructure S004 for filling.
We must fill it with data from first CC only. Is there any problem if the people who create orders, deliveries and billing of second CC work at this time?

A: You can control the updating of infostructure at both header level and tem level using IMG. If you do not want the second company code data to be updated in the info structure, do not include the sales organizations assigned to the second company code in the updating of info structure. For your information, the codes are OVRO and OVRP

Question 18: Posting to Accounts

I am working in a system where someone has changed standard SAP and the SAP standard pro forma invoice. Where is this set? There is no account determination procedure assigned to the document in SD but it is picking up the standard one and posting to accounts.

A: In VOFA check the SD Document category. It should be set to U and the transaction group should be set to 8. Likely these were changed to real invoices. The transaction group tells pro forma invoices not to be posted to accounts. If you have a posting block, wait until someone releases it to accounting in change mode.

Question 19: Error Message Creation

I need a modification to make the system issue an error message when the user enters two sales orders with the same reference to the customer's purchase order. What should I do?

A: In the transaction VOV8 (sales document type definition) under general control put an "A" in the check PO number field. In the transaction OVAH (change system messages) change the message category of V4-115 to "E" from "W".

Question 20: Goods Issue From Negative Stock

I want to issue goods where the Storage location has a negative quantity. The system is not allowing me to make a goods issue. How do I configure this?

A: Follow these steps:

1) OMJ1 - Allow negative stocks - at plant level and at storage location level.
2) MM02 - Plant data/stor.2 - check negative stock in plant.

Question 21: Messages Transaction

What transaction do we use to view all messages including warning messages in SAP?

A: You can view these in transaction code SE91.

Question 22: List Partner Functions in Deliveries

I would like to list the partner functions in a delivery. In which table can I find that information?

A: This information is located in table VBPA.

Question 23: Material Specific Pricing

We have a situation where there will be two pricing procedures and depending upon the materials used, either one of them will get picked up. For example we have a field in customer master that helps determine pricing procedure. Similarly, is there any field in the material master that can determine the pricing procedure determination?

A: The pricing procedure applies to the whole document (header and items). You cannot change it at material (item) level.

Question 24: Account Assignment in SD

There is a configuration setting for SD where you are able to activate the account assignment on both header and item level. The activation will basically open up all the respective cost objects. What setting is this?

A: Use transaction code VKOA

Question 25: Customer Hierarchy

How do you create two customer hierarchies for the same payer?

A: Create an order and delivery, and then perform a PGI for first customer hierarchy. Do the same for the second customer hierarchy.

Question 26: Pricing Procedure

I have created two pricing procedures. One is for normal pricing and the other for taxes. When I am trying to do a sales order, only the first pricing procedure is applying and it is not accepting the second one. Why? What is the exact link between these two pricing procedures and the condition types?

A: The pricing procedure is determined according to: sales area, customer pricing procedure field in the customer master (sold-to), document pricing procedure field in the sales document type. You may need to identify the criteria to determine the right pricing procedure when you enter a sales order. The transaction code to define pricing procedure determination is OVKK. Normally taxes are included in the actual pricing procedure, as part of the determination of the actual price (including taxes) the customer will pay. Taxes need to be calculated based on the given prices in the pricing procedure.

Question 27: Mandatory Condition

While creating quotation, I am getting the error" Mandatory condition MWST is missing." Although MWST is present in procedure RVAA01, what are the steps to solve this?

A: Use transaction code VK11 and enter condition type MWST. Next, enter the details in that document.

Question 28: BOM Usage

When we create a BOM through CS01, what effect does BOM usage field have on subsequent configuration? For example, if we take it as 1=production or 5=sales what effect will it have on subsequent processes?

A: A sales usage means that production will not see it, and a production usage means that sales will not see it. The components each may or may not be saleable, but as a sales BOM is intended to explode onto a sales order, a non-saleable item on a sales BOM would generally not be recommended.

The usage is precisely what it sounds like; which function will use the particular BOM.

Question 29: Copying Text to Other Sales Documents

How do you copy item text from sales order, to delivery, to invoice?

A: Use text control function, SD-> basic function-> text control.

Question 30: Delay Billing

How do you delay billing to the next month in a delivery note?

A: You can postpone the invoice date in the sales order that belongs to that particular delivery under the billing tab. Otherwise by default, the invoice will pick up the GI date of the delivery. If it is acceptable to put the GI on hold until the day of invoicing you could also suggest this as a procedure.

Question 31: Company Code

How should I assign GL account to the company code? I am doing SD/FI Interface. By using transaction code FSSO I am able to enter GL account and company code. But when I try to save it I am getting the error "Account xyz does not exist in company code xyz."

A: You must create the GL account for the company code, exactly like you create a customer master for a CC, or a material in a plant.

Question 32: Customer Invoice Based on MIRO Receipt

When we create a third party customer order, it generates a PO to the vendor. When we receive the vendor invoice, it is entered in MIRO, which then generates an order-related customer invoice. If we create for example, three different sales orders and three separate POs and also make three separate invoice receipts that are done on the same day, these invoices are not combining into a single invoice for the customer. We need this to only be one invoice per sales order. Where is the logic that controls this and how do we change it?

A: You will have to take a look at copy control (from Sales document to Billing document), on item level. Most likely the routine will show 001. If you change that routine to 003, then you should get an invoice per sales order.

Question 33: Sending Invoice via Email

I have a requirement to send the invoice copy to the customer or agent that will be specified at the time of sending the invoice (it should not be configured before). How do I configure this and where do I set the indicators?

A: Use transaction code NACE. Define the output type here. In application V3, define the correct transmission medium. If you want to send it at your convenience select the dispatch time as 3 (Send with applications own transaction). Attach the output type to the correct output determination procedure defined for the document type. Use T Code VF31 to send the message. You will need basis while configuring the email addresses because SCOT and SOST will be used by it.

Question 34: Incomplete delivery for child model (free gift) under BOM

I have a BOM item and another item, which is a free gift for child model. This was not delivered to the dealer, but delivery order status indicates "complete delivery" and the scheduled line appeared fine as well. After my analysis, I found some things. The initial quantity of the BOM item is 5 and free good is 0. How do I go about fixing this?

A: You cannot manipulate and make changes afterwards expecting the system to honor your requirements. You must add the child items as a separate order.

Question 35: SD/FI Interface

A problem occurs while releasing invoice to accounting. Billing is created successfully, but the invoice is not released to accounting. The error message I receive after saving the document states "error in account determination." How should I solve this problem?

A: The first thing you should do is check the account determination log in the invoice.

Follow these steps: transaction code VF02-> Environment-> Acc.determ.analysis-> Revenue Accounts.

Question 36: Number Range Buffering

I am facing a problem in the internal number range assignment of customer data. I have created a new account group and with each customer I create, the system gives an increment of 5. For example it increases from 10005 to 10010 instead of 10005, 10006. How do I fix this?

A: The problem is with the number range buffering. Go to transaction code SNUM, and then object type "debitor." Click on the pencil (change mode) and change the number in buffer.

Question 37: What is a "Characteristic?"

How does the term characteristic relate to transaction code CTO4?

A: Material master leads to classification, and then you select the desired class. Based on class you can choose the characteristics. These characteristics are defined in CT04.

Question 38: Consignment Stock

What process do you use to create a consignment stock?

A: Follow pathway-> SAP Library-> SAP R/3 Enterprise Application Components-> Logistics-> Sales and Distribution (SD)-> Sales-> Special Business Processes in Sales-> Consignment Stock Processing.

Question 39: Excise Tax

What is the business process of excise tax and how do you relate that in SAP?

A: Excise tax is the duty charged on manufacture of goods listed in the chapter and section head of Central Excise Tariff Act. Process should amount to manufacture and separate identifiable finished goods should emerge having marketability and specified in Tariff Act.(?????)

As far as SAP is concerned you, find CIN version integrated with standard SAP from 4.7 onwards. There are two places where you need to configure CIN. The first is Financial Accounting-> Tax on Sale and Purchase and the other is Logistic General-> Tax on Goods Movement.

Question 40: Info Structure

I created a new info structure and activated update rules for it. What is the best way to transport them into a productive system?

A: After rigorous testing in the QA environment and approval of the user community you should transport the info structure and related items into a production environment during "down time," possibly when no billing documents are being created and posted.

Question 41: New Fields in Sales Order

Are there any user exits or any other way to include new fields in the sales order VA01?

A: There are two ways to approach this. You can go to transaction code SE93 and give the Transaction as VA01. It will lead to a screen where you can click on a program that will take you to mod.pool. In this program click Find Icon and key in customer there. It will show you the user exits in that particular program. Another way is using SPRO. Follow path IMG->SD->System Modifications->User Exits. There you can click on the help document and it will show all the user exits with program name. Select the suitable one.

Question 42: Price Adjustment for STO

For STO when the invoice receipt (MM) and invoice issue (SD) is completed, how do we perform a price adjustment if we find the price is incorrect? If we do a subsequent credit/debit in MM, how do we create subsequent credit/debit in SD?

A: First cancel your invoices (SD and MM). Change the price in the STO PO. Then create new invoices SD and MM. The new values will be picked up if properly configured. The difference in the material value will be automatically posted to the appropriate stock account when you create the invoice in MIRO.

Question 43: Variant Configuration

I am making an inquiry in which I have a configurable material. When I create a quotation with reference to the inquiry, the system is not allowing me to change the configuration in the quotation. I checked the copy control and found that at the item level copy control between inquiry and quotation, we have an option for configuration. I have tried these, yet I am still unable to change the configuration. What should I do?

A: The document may already exist. Once fixed you cannot "unfix" the configuration by changing the customizing. You must create a new quote/order. Use setting "A."

Question 44: Output with Different Language

Is it possible to have to have two delivery notes in two different languages?

A: The destination country will decide which language the output should be printed. Make sure that you are identifying that in the program attached to the output and accordingly open the desired form.

Question 45: Text Determination

Can I copy text from the delivery note to the billing document? How can I do this through text determination?

A: You can copy text from Delivery Note to invoice. Go to the IMG (SD>Basic Functions>Text Control) and click on the help icons next to text types. Define access sequences for determining texts and define and assign text determination procedures. You need to check the delivery text field in the relevant billing document type. If you do not check this field you will not be able to copy the delivery texts to the billing document.

Question 46: Intercompany sales

I am working on Intercompany sales. How do I create
material in both company codes?

A: Use transaction code MM01 to create material with
organizational data pertaining to the plants and sales
organizations.

Question 47: Lost Tax Field in Customer Master and Material Master

I do not know why the tax field in the customer master and material master is hidden. This field is not suppressed in customer master. How do I make this field appear?

A: Make sure you have a tax category defined for your countries in OVK1. Then check if the tax classes are defined in OVK3 and OVK4.

Question 48: Shipping Point

On the sales order shipping tab there is a field with the text "shipping point." I would like to add new shipping points to certain plants. Where is this configured in SAP?

A: New shipping points are defined in enterprise structure.
Follow these steps: logistics execution -> define shipping points and assign the shipping point to plant in assign in enterprise structure under logistics execution. Next, click: shipping -> shipping point and good receipt determination. Configure for automatic determination of shipping point based on shipping condition, loading group, and plant. Maintain relevant shipping condition in customer master. Maintain relevant loading group in material master (normally the standard). For the combination that you derive from the sales order, you should have a configuration entry for automatic determination in sales order.

Question 49: Tax Code Determination in Invoicing Document

If several items with different VAT rates are included in one invoice, these different rates are displayed in the invoice header including the respective amount. After saving the invoice, the system determines one VAT rate including one tax code and transfers this tax code to the accounting document. How does this determination work? What is the rule behind this determination?

A: In FS01/02/03 you will see that there is a tax category field where you enter the used tax code for this account. Normally tax conditions have specific account keys. Through transaction code VKOA or OV35 you assign which account (using key fields from sales) will be used for the account doc. Check V08 price procedure for the used account key as well.

Question 50: Cancel Invoice

When a user releases an invoice to accounting it creates an accounting document. The status of the accounting document is cleared if the user cancels this invoice. Is it necessary to delete the previously created accounting document?

A: No, but you will have a credit note in your customer account.

Question 51: LIS Update Terminated After Client Copy

I have a problem with LIS. After client copy, our test system does not update LIS info structures. When I save a sales order, delivery or billing document I receive an error message that says, "update was terminated". How do I fix this?

A: Generate the infostructure and update group again in the client in which you are facing the problem.

Question 52: How to trace changes in sales order

How do you trace the changes made in the sales order in regards to changes to the partner function in the sales order?

A: If you go into the change mode of the sales order click on environment, and then change. This menu will show you that partner functions like SH / BP / PY in the document are changed. It also shows old and new values.

Question 53: STO Delivery Creation List

I am working on cross company STO. After I create STO, I cannot create outbound delivery by using VL10D. When I check the STO, I find that the delivery creation date is blank. It seems the system does not add the STO to delivery due list automatically. Is some setting in SD affecting this?

A: The delivery creation date is blank because the STO is blocked by release strategy.

Question 54: Credit Check

Typically you receive a standard credit check when you save the sales order. What is the best way to trigger it at the start of the sales order creation so that one does not have to enter a lot of data in case you reach the credit limit?

A: The ideal way is to check the credit limit of the customer much before the processing the sales order. Follow the path mentioned within the sales order. Also check: Sales Order-> Environment-> Partners-> Display Credit Account.

Question 55: Printing Several Copies

Is there a way to print an invoice five times?
(One original and four copies)

A: Use transaction code VF02. Once inside the document, click on Go to-> Header ->Output. Select the output type (normally RD00). Click on Communication method and in the field "Number of messages", enter the number of copies you want to print.

Question 56: Order quantity and Confirmed quantity

What is the difference between order quantity and confirmed quantity?

A: The confirmed quantity is the allocated quantity by the availability check (ATP).

Question 57: Subtotals in Pricing

How do the subtotals that have carry over value KOMP-KZWI1, KOMP-KZWi2, work with respect to condition types?

A: Subtotals are not tied to condition types per say. You control what goes into the field by assigning subtotals within you pricing procedure. If you assign a particular line in your pricing procedure to be subtotal 5, its value will be moved to KOMP-KZWI5.

Question 58: Transaction VF04 Authorization Check for Division

When we run the transaction for VF04 no authorization check is done for this division. This is causing some problems because some users run the transaction VF04 and create billing documents for a division for which they are not responsible. Is there a user exit or other way that we can force transaction VF04 to look at the division as part of the authorization check?

A: Make the modification to include a check within the copying requirements of the division in the source document instead of the user authorization.

Question 59: Plant Stock

I have created a new material in SAP, and now wish to add stock for that material into a particular plant. What is the best transaction code as well as movement type to use?

A: Use transaction code MB1C and movement type 561.

Question 60: Create a Condition for Transaction Code VK31

I defined manually a condition type Z004 (as a copy of the condition type K004). I then tried to create condition in transaction code VK31 in the section Discount/Surcharges -> By Material. The system reported, "Table 304 is not defined for use with condition type ZEC1." How should I resolve this?

A: VK31 works with pricing reports. If you want to have a new condition type to be maintainable via VK31 or VK32., you need to do the following: Create pricing report via transaction code V/LA and include the tables you need. Extend the price area menu via SE43. Area menu = COND_AV.

Question 61: Assigning Movement Type

How do I assign movement type?

A: You assign movement type against the schedule line category.

Question 62: Organization Structure

We are implementing R/3 in an auction services company where they have nearly 15 auction services under 5 business units. Our team has two ideas on how to treat the services. One opinion is to treat business units as a distribution channel and service types as divisions. But the problem with this is the sales area number is going up and master data has to be extended across them all. The other idea is to have a dummy distribution channel and have business units as divisions. This way the service types can be treated as sales order types. However it might be difficult to have different pricing for the same order type. What should we do?

A: This must be defined upon how your customer expects the reporting to be. If their expectation is to look on performance by services, then you have to define them as divisions. Defining services as order type is not the right approach, since you face the same problem of data maintenance issues here too, should a service type be moved to a different business unit. Look for the reporting they have today and the reporting expected out of SAP. This will determine which course to take.

Question 63: To View the Invoice Due Date

A certain customer has credit payment terms wherein if the invoice is cut between Dec 1 –15 2005, then the invoice due date should be Jan 15, 2006.
I have configured the payment terms in the transaction code OBB8. I created the sales order with the customer and got the specific payment terms in the overview screen, and then I made the delivery and then the invoice. Can I view the invoice due date (Jan 16,2006) in the invoice?

A: You should be able to see the due date in the AR Module. If you go into fbl5n and search for the customer, you can see the due date in the overview screen.

Question 64: Rejecting and Canceling Sales Order Items

I am in the VA02 transaction for a sales order and want to reject the line items and cancel the entire sales order. What is the menu path needed to achieve this goal?

A: Click the reject document button and then enter a reason for rejection. This will reject the line items and the sales order. You can enter a reason for rejection on the line item sales a tab.

Question 65: Cannot Save Layout under SD01 under 4.5B

Under transaction code SDO1, I try to save a display variant with the pathway: settings-> display variants. However the save option is grayed-out. How should I resolve this issue?

A: There is an unapplied SAP Note that will correct the error. Once the correct note is applied the save option will not be grayed-out.

Question 66: Change of Sales Document

A sales document type of a sales order can be changed after getting saved. How do you do this?

A: One way is through the configuration of document type in transaction code VOV8 (O
Another way is in the "Transaction Flow" section.
You can also perform "Alt sales doc type 1" and "Alt sales doc type 2."

Question 67: Product Allocation Exception

We have set availability check against product allocation using fields Prod.allocation obj., MATNR, WERKS and customer in the referenced infostructure. In the infostructure referenced, these fields are coming from MCVBAP-MATNR, MCVBAP-WERKS. But for the structure field "plant," we now need to make an exception. In certain cases we have to check and update existing allocation in a plant different from the delivering plant. I found EXIT_SAPLQUOT_003 to check allocation on a different plant, but I am not able to find a way to update the structure on this plant. Do I have to change the update rules/source fields for the infostructure?

A: The user exit is only useful for changing the plant prior to executing product allocation checks. To get the update of the infostructure against the same plant, you will need to write a routine for the plant in the infostructure.

Question 68: Default distribution channel

We have only one distribution channel in our company. Can we default it in the transaction field that needs distribution channel data? How can we configure that?

A: You can use the user master data to achieve this. Use transaction code SU01 and input the user ID. Go to the parameters tab page and add parameter VTW. Input your default distribution channel in the parameter value. The only drawback with this method is you will have to individually do this for all your users.

Question 70: Third Party Sales Order Scenario

On plant P1 a sales order is created which is converted into PR and PO. A central purchasing plant P2 processes it and sends it to the vendor. Vendor supplies goods to plant P2. P2 then transfers the goods to P1. P1 then delivers it to customer. We want actual plant to do the goods receipt. Meaning P2 would receive the stock initially for sales order (TAB) and linked purchase order (having plant P1) if goods are coming to P2. Subsequently, when P2 plant delivers the sales order stock to P1 plant, P1 should create the goods receipt for stock transfer delivery. The reason we want to achieve this is so not to disturb the material costs, as once the goods are received it will be valuated. How do we do this?

A: You could have the requirement placed on P1, which then creates a dependent requirement on P2. When purchased, it is sent to P2. The dependent requirement causes a STO between P1 and P2, and the customer demand requires fulfillment out of P1.

Question 71: Automatic Packing

I want to use automatic packing and I have to create the procedure for packing instructions. Where and how can I link the procedure with my delivery type or item category?

A: The procedure is assigned in transaction OVHU2. You will have to assign the procedure to 0002 Outbound Delivery. Here you cannot specify the delivery type or item category. To some extent, you can control this with the packing indicator in the delivery item category, however, you can have better control by designing the access sequence with the available fields.

Question 71: Availability Check

Is it possible to perform an availability check based on the plant yet exclude one storage location?

A: You can make a storage location not available to the availability check in MM.

Question 72: Copying text

Is it possible to copy texts from sales order header to billing document header?

A: Use transaction VOTXN, and then create an access sequence with text object VBBK. Also make sure that the requirement of access sequence is given as '1'-Ref doc. Header.

Question 73: Customer stock in the MD04

I must create an order. Whenever a sales order is created in the schedule line items, the check box "Fixed date and quantity" is checked. In the MD04 transaction, customer requirements for the sales order are not appearing. Why is this?

A: Regarding fix date and quantity check box check transaction OVZJ for your sales area. With the second problem regarding MD04, you must check two things; requirements class and scheduling category. Check your document to see whether they are activated for requirement transfer.

Question 74: Printing Customer Details

In transaction XD03 we can print details for a single customer. Is there any transaction code to print all the customers' address or details at one time?

A: For this requirement check TC: S_ALR_87012179 & S_ALR_87012180.

Question 75: Table for Sales Organization

What table do I use in creating ABAP program that would output the sales based on sales organization of customers?

A: If you have SIS update turned on, you can use transaction code MTCE against infostructure 001 to display sales by sales organization and so forth. Apart from SIS, you may create simple ABAP query with LDB VAV. If you want to create an ABAP report only, then use transaction code VBRK ->billing header table and VBRP ->billing item table.

SAP SD Fundamentals

SAP Sales and Distribution Processing Document Flow

Document Flow in Sales

The sales documents you create are individual documents but they can also form part of a chain of inter-related documents. For example, you may record a customer's telephone inquiry in the system. The customer next requests a quotation, which you then create by referring to the inquiry. The customer later places an order on the basis of the quotation and you create a sales order with reference to the quotation. You ship the goods and bill the customer. After delivery of the goods, the customer claims credit for some damaged goods and you create a free-of-charge delivery with reference to the sales order. The entire chain of documents – the inquiry, the quotation, the sales order, the delivery, the invoice, and the subsequent delivery free of charge – creates a document flow or history. The flow of data from one document into another reduces manual activity and makes problem resolution easier. Inquiry and quotation management in the Sales Information System help you to plan and control your sales.

The following graphic shows how the various types of sales documents are inter-related and how data subsequently flows into shipping and billing documents

Sales Document Type

Sales document can have many different document type. Each document type has its own usage..

Some commonly used document types are:-

+ OR - Standard Order
+ RE - Returns
+ FD - Delivery Free of Charge

Different Sales Document types have different control parameters.

For e.g. Document type ZOWN :-

General control :-
Check Division -
Blank -> no checks
    1 -> Dialog to inform user that the division is different from material master
    2 -> Error when division is different from material master

Shipping
Immediate Delivery
Blank -> Create delivery separately
    1 -> Create delivery immediately when sales order is save
    2 -> Create delivery if quantity can be confirmed to day

Maintain Sales Document Type

+ Transaction VOV8 - Double click on the document type to check the configuration.

Some configurations you can specify:-

+ Check credit limit
+ Define the default Delivery type
+ Define the default Billing type
+ Block the Document Type from being used etc.

New Division/Sales Area/Sales Office

4.6x

OVXA - Assign division to sales organization
OVXG - Set up sales area

OVXM - Assign sales office to sales area
e.g. Sales Organization -> Distribution Channel ->
Division

> |
> -> Sales Office

VOR2 - Define Common Divisions

OVAN - Combine divisions allows you to share sales document type data between different divisions. You define the sales document types in a central division and then use it as a reference division.
For e.g.

Sales Organization	Division	Reference division
ALL	01	01
ALL	02	01
ALL	03	01

OVKK - Define Pricing Procedure Determination
For e.g.
Sales Organization   Distribution
Channel   Division   Document
Procedure   Pricing Procedure

ALL		01	01
A	1		

SM30 Table/View :
V_TSPA   - Define New Division
V_T134G_WS   - Assign Business Area To Plant
V_TVTA_GRE - Define Rules By Sales Area
V_TVTA_KFV - Assign business area by sales area
V_TVAKZ   - Assign sales order types permitted for sales areas

What is the difference between sales organization and sales area?

Organizational Structure broadly refers to the way a company follows a set path of systems/hierarchies.
Different companies do have different structures and the differences in structures emanates basically from the strategies.

Sales organization is the organizational unit which responsible for the selling of the product, movement of goods to the customer.

Sales Area is the combination of the Sales: Organization + Distribution Channel + Division.

Company code of an organization is the legal entity which have separate Balance sheet and profit & loss A/C required by law for the legal purpose so whenever an organizational unit have different Balance sheet and P/L A/c you can define a company code.

A Company's structure can be mapped in R/3 which would facilitate flow of information, flow of process and also facilitates work flow in a logical way.

A Sales organization structure is based on the Elements of the Organization which are as follows.

1. Company Code
2. Sales Organization
3. Distribution Channel
4. Division
5. Plant
6. Shipping Point.

A Company Code is generally created by finance and it broadly represents the highest point of structure.

The relationship between Sales Org and Company code is Unique. One Sales Organization can be assigned to one Company code. Think of one practical situation where in u can Say that Essar is One Group (Client).
Essar Infotech (Company Code), Essar Oil (Company Code).
Essar Oil may have Essar South (Sales Org) and Essar North(Sales Org). You have to remember that Essar South is only assigned to Essar Oil and not Essar Infotech right....

A Combination of Sales Org, Distribution Channel and Division is called a Sales Area and a Sales Area is assigned to the company thru the Sales Orgn.

A plant is assigned to the company code. It is also assigned to the Sales Org and Dist Channel and this channel is called Delivering Plant.

A Shipping Point is assigned to the CLIENT.

Block Sales Document Type / Delivery / Billing by Customer

When there is a temporarily stop of business with a customer, you can block new orders to be created for this customer. You can have the options of blocking all the work flow or let the delivery and billing to continue for any open orders.

VD05 - Block/Unblock Customer

OVAS - Sales Order Type Blocking reasons
OVAL - Blocking reasons links with Sales Order Type

OVZ7 - Delivery Blocking reasons
OVV3 - Billing Blocking reasons

In 4.6x, if you found that your Sales Order Billing Block is not working, it is because you need to build the Billing Block for the Billing Type.

SM30 - Table/View V_TVFSP

If you want a material to be blocked, go to the Basic data 1 view of the material, there in the general data you have " X-plant material status ". Also in Cost estimate 1 view of the material you have Plant Specific Material status. Use the options available to block the material in these two views.

You cannot use the material in sales order

Use the material exclusion function:

FUNCTIONALITY:
SD> Master data > Products > Listing/Exclusion>
Create
(Transaction codes VBO1, VBO2, VBO3)

Enter the list/exclusion type B001: For the
required

Customer:
Enter Maintain materials > Save > Exit

Create the order and enter material excluded to test
exclusion.

CONFIGURATION: IMG SETTINGS
For IMG settings; Go to IMG > SD > Basic
Functions>Listing/Exclusion

Ensure that the listing/exclusion procedure is
activated for your order type. You can also create
your own condition types access sequences and
procedures or use the SAP provided ones.

Wrong/duplicate RE Created

+ Check Document Flow for RE
  Decision:-
    o No Goods Issue and No Credit Memo created
    o Reject the sales order item
    o No Goods Issue and Credit Memo created
      ▪ Cancel Credit Memo
      ▪ Reject the sales order item
    o Goods Issue and Credit Memo created
    o Create another OR to offset the credit memo created. Treat this as a normal OR process. Ensure that account receivable is informed by typing in the item text. Please do not send invoice to customer as the RE is wrongly/duplicate.

Note: When you create another OR, the delivery department may actually go and delivery the goods to customer. Thus, it is important to inform them that this OR is for internal adjustment. The process of posting the goods issue must be done by the delivery side for proper flow.

Movement type determination and Availability

SM30 - Table View - V_TVEPZ -> Assign schedule line categories

+ First check the Proposed schedule line category (SchLC) - double click on the line item

VOV6 - Maintain the schedule line categories - double click on the line item

+ For example, you can control the default returns movement type.
+ 651 - two steps - with a transfer posting using 453
+ 653 - one steps - direct post to unrestricted used

Control the Transaction Flow (tick to activate the function)

+ transfer of requirement
+ for availability check for sales
+ production allocation active

Sales reservation

Sales reservation takes place automatically through availability check

The setting is on the checking group (OVZ2 - Define Checking Groups).
You must set the "Accumul." column. Without setting this it will only check availability but not reserve it!

SAP recommend Accumul. = 3 -> Accumulate the requirements quantity when creating and accumulate the confirmed quantity when making changes.

For manual reservation, you can use MB21, movement type 251 - Goods Issue for sales.
To activate the Sales Order number field, do the followings :-
Activate transaction OMBW
double click movement type 251
double click additional acct. assign.
Tick the required/optional button as per your requirement.

The user has to manage the manual reservation using MBVR.

Reserving material without sales order

In Order to reserve the specific materials for a particular customer, use Strategy 50 to plan your MRP with the materials getting reserved for customer when you make Individual / Collective requirement (1) in MRP4 view of Material Master

Or you can create a manual reservation against that particular material and give the customer name in the Recipient Field so that you can easily identify the Material which belong to the Customer

Sales Order Stock

Sales Order Stock is stock with Special Stock type E. It can fall into the usual stock categories such as unrestricted, blocked etc. but "belongs" to a sales order. For example, you create a sales order for a part and assign a sales item category that generates an individual requisition, the requirement has an account assignment linking it to the sales order schedule line, and you convert that requisition to a Purchase Order.

When you receive the Purchase Order, the stock is placed in sales order stock. It will show against the sales order/sales order line. It can only be delivered against that sales order line. Any availability check etc for that material on any other sales order will not take it into account as it is not available except to the sales order line the stock is assigned to.

Forecasted and Confirmed Sales Orders

MD73 - Display Total Requirements

Enter the material or MRP controller you want to analyze.

Assignment field options:

1. If you with to look at how the planned independent requirements have been match to the sales order. Sales order which are over and above that forecasted are not shown.
2. If you are interested primarily in seeing what sales order are over and above the sales forecast.
3. If you are interested in seeing all the sales order with indication of whether or not they have been anticipated in the forecast.
4. If you wish to see all the three reports of the above three options together. Blank if you with to see a complete list of sales order, without any indication of whether they have been anticipated in the forecast.

Backorder Processing

Backorder processing is a piece of functionality in SAP where you can change the commitments and over-ride the blockage of stock marked against sales documents/deliveries. For example, you receive an order from a very important customer for material "A" but the entire quantity of A is committed to another customer "B" via earlier sales orders and this is where BACKORDER processing helps you to change the commitment and shift stock due for B to A. This is the benefit of this functionality.

OMIH - Checking rule for updating backorders
OPJL - Define new checking rule
OPJJ   - Define scope of check

V_RA - Backorder Processing

Data selection:-
Sold-to-party   Customer code   Mandatory
Sales Organization   Mandatory
Distribution Channel   Mandatory
Division   Mandatory

Changed confirmed quantity :-
Tick the material you want to change and click the Backorder button
Confirmed quantity that still can be changed are highlighted.

V.15 - Backorder List
Sales Organization   Mandatory

Distribution Channel	Mandatory
Division	Mandatory

Third Party Order Processing

Third party order processing is as follows:

Assume three companies X, Y and Z
X - The company,
y - The customer
Z - Vendor

When ever X gets a PO from Y to supply some goods; X has an option of either manufacturing those goods or procuring those goods.

If he is procuring the goods, there are two methods that are generally followed:

Method 1) After receiving the PO from Y, X creates a sales order against Y.
Now at the same time he also creates a PO to a vendor Z to produce the goods
Z produces the goods and supplies to X
X receives the goods from Z
Then X delivers the same goods to Y.
After that X invoices Y and Z invoices X.

Note : Here there is no direct/ Indirect relation between Z and Y.

This process is known as Trading Process. And the Material here is created with Material type HAWA.

The other method is a Third party order processing method:

Here the glaring difference is that instead of Z supplying the material to X and X in turn supplying the same material to Y.

X authorizes Z to supply the material to Y on his behalf and notify him once the delivery is complete.

Now Z supplies the material to Y and acknowledges the same to X.

Z will send a copy of delivery acknowledgement and invoice to X.

After receiving the delivery confirmation and invoice from Z, X has to verify the invoice and this process is known as invoice verification and is done in SAP through Transaction code MIRO.

The next step for X is to create an invoice and submit to Y. Only after the invoice verification document is posted then only X can create an invoice for Y. This is the business flow that is followed for third party order configuration. There are few steps that have to be configured to enable the system to function as mentioned above.

1. If you are always following a third party process for a material then you have to create the material using item category group BANS.

The procurement type should be marked as External procurement (F) in MRP 2 view of the material master record.

If you are not always allowing third party order processing then u can create a material master record with item category group as NORM and the procurement type should be marked as (X) meaning both types of procurement (in house manufacturing and external procurement).

2. The item category in the order should be manually changed as TAS. For that you need to configure the item category determination

ord type + item cat grp + usage + Hiv level = Item cat + Manual item cat

OR + NORM +   +   = TAN . + TAS
OR + BANS +   +   = TAS

3. Make sure that during the item category configuration for TAS you need to mark relevant for billing indicator as F

4. The schedule line category for this type should be CS. Make sure that you mark subsequent type as NB - purchase requisition in this schedule line category as this will trigger the purchase requisition order immediately after the creation of the sales order and the PO to vendor is created against this purchase requisition.

Product Group and Sales BOM

My client collects products with quantities in something they call Product Group. The customer calls in and orders for the product group and automatically gets in all the associated materials.

Do we need a Sales Order BOM to handle this?

This is a good example of a Sales Order BOM. But the configuration of Sales BOM depends upon certain conditions like:

If you want to create the product group and price it at header level or if you want to assemble the products and depending upon the assemblies you want to price .

For example, if the customer asks for a certain combination of Material A, B and C respectively, then you create a Material Master record Material D with item category group as LUMF.

While the Materials A, B and C are created with standard item category groups NORM only.

Then create a sales BOM using Transaction code CS01 and enter the following details:

Material : Material D
Plant : Plant in which you created the material.
BOM Usage : 5 (Sales and Distribution)

then give the Materials A, B, and C and give their respective quantities.

Before you have to create pricing condition records for Materials A, B, and C.

Then configure the item categories (T - code : VOV4).

When processing the sales order, just give the Material D and the system will pick up the corresponding assemblies for that material and populate in the order.

The item category for the header item will be TAP and the item category for the items will be TAN,

In this case the Material D is called as the higher level Item , and all the assemblies are called as the sub items.

Here the sub items are relevant for pricing and delivery where as the header item is not relevant for neither pricing nor delivery. It just acts as a text item.

This type of configuration of BOM is known as pricing at item level. This is used when you don't know what quantities of assemblies the customer is going to order and if the price of the assembly keeps varies.

There is another way of configuring BOM which is pricing at header level.
The difference is that the Material Master D has to be configured using the item category group ERLA.

Creation of BOM is same.

But you need to maintain the pricing condition record for the header item.

The item categories in this case would be
Header item : TAQ
Sub item TAE;

Where the header item is relevant for pricing and delivery. And sub items are not relevant for neither the pricing nor the delivery.

Depending upon your requirements you can configure accordingly.

Defining Company and Assigning Sales Organization

Definition of Company Code

1.Transaction Code: SPRO
2. Click Enterprise IMG button
3. Select Enterprise Structure -> Definition -> Financial Accounting -> Define, Copy, Delete, Check Company Code -> Edit Company Code Data
4. Check the check box and all yes radio buttons. Click Continue button
5. Click New Entries Button and Type your company code and name.

Assignment of Sales Organization to Company Code
1. Transaction Code: SPRO
2. Click Enterprise IMG button
3. Select Enterprise Structure -> Assignment -> Sales and Distribution -> Assign Sales Organization to Company Code

Joy

The sales organization is an organizational unit within logistics, which structures the company according to its sales requirements. It represents the selling unit as a legal entity. It is responsible for product guarantees and other rights to recourse, for example. Regional subdividing of the market can also be carried out with the help of sales organizations.

Each business transaction is processed within a sales organization.

Each sales organization is assigned exactly one company code for which you enter all accounting details of the sales organization.

A distribution chain can be active for several plants and the plants can be assigned to different company codes. If the sales organization and plant are assigned to different company codes, an internal billing document is sent between the company codes before the sales transactions are entered for accounting purposes.

Partner Procedures

Sold-to-party (Customer Master) - Payment, Tax determination

Bill-to-party - Address to send the invoice to
Ship-to-party - Deliver the goods to
Payer - Pay to who (a company/person name)

VOPA - Maintain Partner Determination

Click Partner Object

Click Partner Procedures

Double Click on the Procedures Line Items

To pass the partner function contact person (CP) data to the ship-to-party in the delivery document.

Go to the Partner Determination procedure for you sales order type. Look for the column that is labeled SOURCE.
Put SH against partner function CP and it will assign CP from ship-to-party to afterwards.

As long as you have CP in your delivery document, it will be copied from SO to Delivery properly

One Time Customer

V-07 - Create a one-time customer. (Account Group - CPDA)

In order for the user to create sales order, you have to maintain the Account group for the Sold-to Party. (SP) VOPA - Maintain Partner Determination

Click Partner functions

Click Environment -> Account Group. Assignment

To create a new entry, press Page Down till the last line.

Goods Return from Customer

We have posted GI to ship the material from our plant to our customer plant in Japan (also belongs to our own company, we're doing intercom transfer). Now they want to return the material to us.

What is the process for us to do goods Return? What are the exact steps/transactions used to handle this process.

What if the billing document has been created and they have made payment to us?

What if the billing document has been created and sent but they have made payment to us?

A: All returns against sales order are affected against sales order type RE.

You can copy this order type and rename it to suit your purpose. Kindly understand that sales returns are against billing raised. This means while creating the sales return order, that it will be created with reference to the Billing Number. This will ensure all the original effects in the billing to be passed on to the SRA . The credit memo is based on the order and not on the delivery.

Try this first in the development server before doing it in the production server. Also, ensure to verify that the credit memo actually credits the customer and debits sales account. We had this problem due to some hot patch application in version 4.0B and then had to get the relevant code from SAP OSS for applying in the copy control routines. As regards the payment, the amount will appear as credit balance in the customer account and you need to decide whether to adjust against some other invoice or refund the amount to the party.

You won't be able to use the standard customer return process for these cases. A customer return will only do the postings on one side (goods receipt, customer credit memo), but will not reduce inventory on the other side or create the debit memo. I had the same requirement in a previous project and we used the same process we had for the initial transactions, just everything starts from your plant in Japan and they deliver stock to your plant and charge you.

SD Customer Master Tables

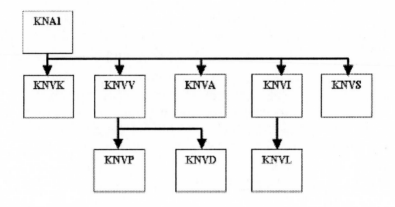

Rebate Agreement and Partner Determination

How do I create and process a Rebate agreement? Why is partner determination so important and also explain the procedure for Partner determination?

Following explains how to create a rebate agreement, test it using a sales order and billing it. Then settling it partially or fully using a rebate credit memo. Please use the basic procedure and tweak your IMG settings according to your unique requirements.

Rebate processing:
1. First requirement is that the rebate processing must be active for
a. the customer (check in customer master) ,
b. for the billing type (check in IMG > Billing > rebate processing > active rebate processing > select billing documents for rebate processing.)
c. For the sales organization:
   (check in IMG > Billing> rebate processing > active rebate processing > Active rebate processing for sales org.)

2. Next create a rebate agreement for this use T-code VB01. For the rebate agreement type you can choose either 0001 (group rebate) or 0002 material rebate or 0003 (customer rebate), etc. b. Enter your rebate conditions. Don't forget to enter the accrual rate here.

3. Now test your rebate functionality : create a sales order for the particular customer, sales org (ensure that the billing type used in your sales order is relevant for rebate) . Create outbound delivery, transfer order to do picking and post goods issue.

4. Now go to transaction code VB03 and check your rebate by choosing conditions , selecting the condition line and choosing payment data. You will see that the accruals and business volume are updated when accounting doc is created for billing.

5. Settling your rebates:
Once your rebates have been accrued you need to settle the rebate. For this first release the rebate for settlement by using transaction code VB02. As a trial basis choose B (you can choose other settings based on your requirement) and choose Create manual accrual. Now enter the amount to be paid and save the rebate agreement.

6. Next display your rebate agreement using Transaction code VB03. Enter your rebate agreement number . Next choose rebate payments > Rebate documents and select partial settlement. Click on the choose button to note down your credit request number.

7. Use transaction code VA02 and release the billing block for your credit request. (Use item overview tab)

8. Now use VF01 to create a rebate credit memo by entering the credit memo request number and save it

9. Now release the credit memo to accounting using vfo2.

Document Flow in Sales

The sales documents you create are individual documents but they can also form part of a chain of inter-related documents. For example, you may record a customer's telephone inquiry in the system. The customer next requests a quotation, which you then create by referring to the inquiry. The customer later places an order on the basis of the quotation and you create a sales order with reference to the quotation. You ship the goods and bill the customer. After delivery of the goods, the customer claims credit for some damaged goods and you create a free-of-charge delivery with reference to the sales order. The entire chain of documents – the inquiry, the quotation, the sales order, the delivery, the invoice, and the subsequent delivery free of charge – creates a document flow or history. The flow of data from one document into another reduces manual activity and makes problem resolution easier. Inquiry and quotation management in the Sales Information System help you to plan and control your sales.

The following graphic shows how the various types of sales documents are inter-related and how data subsequently flows into shipping and billing documents.

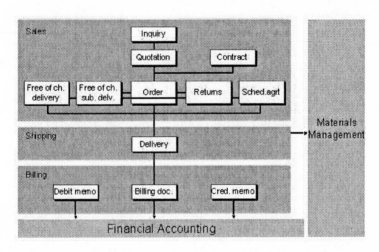

Transaction Code Listing

1. VS00 - Master data
2. VC00 - Sales Support
3. VA00 - Sales
4. VL00 - Shipping
5. VT00 - Transportation
6. VF00 - Billing

Others as follows:
At Configuration:
1. VOV8 - Define Sales documents type (header)
2. OVAZ - Assigning Sales area to sales documents type
3. OVAU - Order reasons
4. VOV4 - Assign Item categories (Item category determination)
5. VOV6 - Schedule line categories
6. OVAL - To assign blocks to relevant sales documents type
7. OVLK - Define delivery types
8. V/06 - Pricing
9. V/08 - Maintain pricing procedure
10. OVKP - Pricing proc determination
11. V/07 - Access sequence

End user:
1. Customer Master Creation-VD01 and XD01 (for full including company code)
   VD02 - Change Customer
   VD03 - Display Customer
   VD04 - Customer Account Changes
   VD06 - Flag for Deletion Customer

XD01 - Create Customer
XD02 - Modify Customer
XD03 - Display Customer
2. Create Other material ----MM00
3. VB11- To create material determination condition record
4. CO09- Material availability Overview
5. VL01 - Create outbound delivery with ref sales order
6. VL04 - Collective processing of delivery
7. VA11 - Create Inquiry
   VA12 - Change Inquiry
   VA13 - Display Inquiry

Sales & Distribution
Sales order / Quote / Scheduling Agreement / Contract

· VA01 - Create Order
· VA02 - Change Order
· VA03 - Display Order
· VA02 - Sales order change
· VA05 - List of sales orders
· VA32 - Scheduling agreement change
· VA42 - Contract change
· VA21 - Create Quotation
· VA22 - Change Quotation
· VA23 - Display Quotation

Billing
· VF02 - Change billing document
· VF11 - Cancel Billing document
· VF04 - Billing due list
· FBL5N - Display Customer invoices by line
· FBL1N - Display Vendor invoices by line

Delivery
· VL02N - Change delivery document
· VL04 - Delivery due list
· VKM5 - List of deliveries
· VL06G - List of outbound deliveries for goods issue
· VL06P - List of outbound deliveries for picking
· VL09 - Cancel goods issue
· VT02N - Change shipment
· VT70 - Output for shipments

General
· VKM3, VKM4 - List of sales documents
· VKM1 - List of blocked SD documents
· VD52 - Material Determination

Most Important Tables

KONV Conditions for Transaction Data
KONP Conditions for Items
LIKP Delivery Header Data
LIPS Delivery: Item data
VBAK Sales Document: Header Data
VBAP Sales Document: Item Data
VBBE Sales Requirements: Individual Records
VBEH Schedule line history
VBEP Sales Document: Schedule Line Data
VBFA Sales Document Flow
VBLB Sales document: Release order data
VBLK SD Document: Delivery Note Header
VBPA Sales Document: Partner
VBRK Billing: Header Data
VBRP Billing: Item Data
VBUK Sales Document: Header Status and Administrative Data
VBUP Sales Document: Item Status
VEKP Handling Unit - Header Table
VEPO Packing: Handling Unit Item (Contents)
VEPVG Delivery Due Index

INDEX

Printed in the United States
50224LVS00002B/19

9 781933 804040